CLEAR MONEY, CLEAR MIND

Turning Small Steps Into Big Wins

Mohammed Rahish

CONTENTS

Title Page
Introduction
Emergency Fund   1
Saving   7
Investing   13
Insurance   21
Debt Free   25
CONCLUSION   29

INTRODUCTION

This book is a beginner's guide to personal finance, designed for those who are not familiar with money management. Personal finance is different for everyone because we all have unique perspectives and needs when it comes to managing money.

In this book, you will learn the basics of money management and how to take control of your finances. We'll explore simple and effective ways to manage your money and introduce you to different types of assets available in the world—many of which people aren't aware of.

By the end of this book, you'll have the knowledge and awareness you need to start managing your finances confidently and independently.

EMERGENCY FUND

*"Your Safety Net for
Uncertain Times"*

When I was a teenager, I was obsessed with money. I was a topper in school, but I realized later that my education didn't teach me much about managing it. Subjects like personal finance or money management were never part of our school curriculum.

By the time I finished college and started earning, managing money felt like stepping into a completely new world. I had no idea where to begin. It was overwhelming at first, but this lack of knowledge pushed me to learn more about financial skills. One of the most important lessons I learned was the value of building an emergency fund.

An emergency fund is essential—it's your safety net for life's uncertainties. If you're the sole breadwinner in your family and have just started earning, creating this fund should be your top priority. Life is unpredictable; layoffs, unexpected expenses, or emergencies can strike at any time. Having 6–12 months' worth of expenses saved can give you peace of mind and financial stability in tough times.

Trust me, you won't regret starting your emergency fund today. It's the foundation of a secure financial future for you and your loved ones.
Now that we understand the importance of having an emergency fund, let's talk about how to get started and when to use it.

When Should You Use Your Emergency Fund?
Here's a quick way to figure it out:

Imagine two scenarios:

"You're planning a trip. You've been eyeing your emergency fund and thinking of dipping into it to cover the expenses."

"A family member is unexpectedly hospitalized, and you need money to cover the medical bills."

Take a moment to decide—when is it appropriate to use your emergency fund?

Clearly, the second scenario is the right choice. An emergency fund is meant for unforeseen, urgent situations like medical emergencies, job loss, or unexpected repairs. It's your safety net for moments when life takes an unexpected turn.

On the other hand, using it for personal goals like vacations doesn't count as an emergency. Trips and other non-essential expenses can be planned and saved for separately. We'll explore how to save for personal goals in future chapters on saving and investing.

Reserve your emergency fund for genuine emergencies. By doing so, you ensure it's there when you truly need it.

Now lets talk about How we can actually achieve to set up our first emergency fund.

Set a Realistic Goal:

Start small. Aim for 1-2 months of essential expenses initially, then build up to 6-12 months over time.

Calculate your monthly needs, including rent, utilities, groceries, transportation, and insurance.

Open a Separate Savings Account:

Use a high-yield savings account to store your emergency fund, so it earns some interest but remains easily accessible.

Make Saving a Habit:

Automate a portion of your salary to go directly into the emergency fund. Start with 10–20% of your income or whatever you can afford.

Earn Extra Money:

Consider freelance work, part-time gigs, or selling unused items to accelerate your savings.

Avoid Using It for Non-Emergencies:

Stick to the rule: only use the fund for genuine emergencies, not for vacations or luxury purchases.

Review and Adjust Regularly:

Reassess your goal every year or after significant life changes like marriage, having kids, or buying a home.

> *Don't stress about reaching your goal overnight. Consistency is key. Even small amounts, saved regularly, can grow into a solid financial safety net over time. Start today—you'll thank yourself later!*

❖ ❖ ❖

SAVING

" The Art of Saving and Smart Budgeting "

Budgeting is a crucial skill everyone should learn. Without it, you might find yourself spending money without knowing where it's going, and by the end of the month, you'll be left wondering why your account is empty. This cycle can repeat every month, leaving you feeling clueless and frustrated.

But once you learn how to budget, you'll see a big change. At first, it may feel boring, but trust me, it's a game changer. Once you get the hang of it, you'll enjoy tracking your spending, knowing exactly where your money is going, and where it's coming from.

How Budgeting Helps You:

Let's say your monthly expenses are 30,000, and your income is 50,000. With proper budgeting, you can save 20,000 each month for your goals.

The key is to first understand your expenses in detail. Everyone's financial situation is different, so you need to look at your own spending patterns to come up with a realistic budget.

Once you've broken down your expenses, it's important to stick to your budget. This will help you save more, reduce unnecessary spending, and make sure you're not running out of money unexpectedly.

Remember, budgeting is the first step towards financial control and achieving your goals. You'll feel more confident about your money once you know exactly where it's going!

Suppose, as we discussed earlier, your monthly expenses are 30,000. The goal is to stick to this amount and avoid any unnecessary or additional spending. By staying disciplined and sticking to your budget, you'll ensure that you don't overspend and can save more each month.

Saving and budgeting go hand in hand. Saving is essentially what remains after deducting your expenses from your income:

Saving = Income – Expenses

In other words, no matter how much you earn, saving depends on your ability to budget effectively and control your spending. Let's look at an example. Imagine someone earning 50,000 per month. With disciplined budgeting and avoiding unnecessary expenses beyond their fixed costs, they can save significantly. By the fifth month, they could comfortably save as much as 100,000. This demonstrates how proper budgeting directly supports saving goals and financial growth.

Month	Income	Expense	Saving
Month1	50000	30000	20000
Month2	70000	30000	40000
Month3	90000	30000	60000
Month4	110000	30000	80000
Month3	130000	30000	100000

If someone isn't consistent with budgeting, they might end up with no savings at all.

Now lets see why saving is an important factor in finance,

importance of saving

Saving isn't only for emergencies. It's the first step toward achieving your dreams. Whether it's buying your dream home, going back to school, starting a business, or even taking that once-in-a-lifetime trip, saving helps turn your plans into reality. Every small amount you set aside gets you closer to the things you truly want in life.

There's also the freedom that comes with saving. Without savings, people often rely on credit cards or loans when unexpected expenses arise. This can lead to debt and the stress of repayment. But when you save, you're in control. You don't have to depend on anyone else to meet your needs or chase after your goals.

Saving doesn't just stop at meeting goals or emergencies—it's how you build wealth. When you save and invest, your money starts working for you. Over time, it grows, thanks to something called compound interest. This is when the money you save earns interest, and then that interest earns interest, too. The earlier you start saving, the more powerful this effect becomes.

Inflation, or the rising cost of living, is another reason to save. Prices tend to go up over time, and if you're not saving or investing, the money you have today might not stretch as far tomorrow. Saving helps you stay ahead, ensuring your future remains comfortable even as the world changes.

And then there's retirement. It might feel like it's a long way off, but saving early for your later years makes all the difference. It's what allows you to stop working one day and still live comfortably, doing the things you love without financial stress. Starting early means you'll have more time to grow your savings, making your retirement years truly golden.

Let's not forget the sense of empowerment that saving brings. Knowing you have money set aside gives you confidence. You're no longer at the mercy of life's uncertainties. Instead, you're prepared, ready to face whatever comes your way.

And then there are the opportunities. Sometimes life presents unexpected chances—maybe to start a business, help a loved one, or take on a new adventure. If you've saved, you can grab those opportunities without hesitation. Savings give you the freedom to say "yes" to the things that matter most.

In the end, saving is about creating a life where you feel secure and free. It's not about denying yourself enjoyment today; it's about ensuring you can enjoy both today and tomorrow. With every rupees you save, you're building a better, more stable future—one where you're in charge of your choices and your dreams.

INVESTING

" A Guide to Investing Across Asset Classes "

I began investing from my first job, but at first, I was uncertain about the world of investing. It felt like gambling, and I was afraid to put my hard-earned money into something I wasn't sure about.

To ease myself into it, I started with a small amount in mutual funds. As I saw the returns, my confidence grew, and I started learning more about stocks, mutual funds, intraday trading, and more.

What I've learned from my investment journey is that the earlier you start, the more time your money has to compound. Compounding is often referred to as the eighth wonder of the world, and we will explore this concept in the upcoming chapters.

so lets consider a person age is 23 years old and he starts investing monthly of 10,000 rupees and he keeps investing till the age of 60 and decides to stop investing.

on the other hand a person of age 30 years old and he also invest 10,000 rupees and keeps investing it till the age of he retires that is by the age of 60, Now whom do you think has more money all this year.

Person 1 invests for a longer duration (37 years), while Person 2 invests for a shorter period (30 years). Although Person 2 invests less money in total, Person 1 benefits from 7 more years of compounding.

That's why starting early with investments can be beneficial, as the power of compounding begins to work in your favor.

By now, you must have understood the importance of investing. Let's explore the different asset classes available for starting your investment journey and discuss which ones are suitable based on your age.

As you embark on this journey, it's crucial to understand the various asset classes available and how to effectively allocate your investments according to your age, risk tolerance, and long-term goals. In this book, we will explore each asset class, discuss their characteristics, and guide you on how to approach your investments at different stages of life.

Common Asset Classes for Investment:

Equities (Stocks): Stocks represent ownership in a company, and they offer the potential for high returns, but they come with higher risk. This asset class is best suited for younger investors who have a long-term investment horizon and can tolerate market volatility. The potential return is high, but remember, with great returns comes great risk.

Mutual Funds: Mutual funds pool money from multiple investors to invest in a diversified portfolio of stocks, bonds, or other securities. They are an ideal choice for beginners or those who want a professionally managed investment that offers diversification without requiring direct management. Risk levels vary depending on the type of fund, but the potential for moderate to high returns makes mutual funds a versatile investment tool.

Bonds: Bonds are debt instruments where you lend money to the government or a corporation in return for fixed interest payments over a specific period. This asset class is perfect for conservative investors looking for stability and lower risk. Bonds offer steady returns, though the potential return is usually moderate compared to stocks.

Real Estate: Investing in physical properties or real estate funds (REITs) allows you to hold tangible assets that can generate income through rental income or property appreciation. Real estate offers moderate to high returns depending on the location and type of property. This asset class provides a good balance between income and long-term growth potential.

Gold and Precious Metals: Gold and other precious metals serve as a hedge against inflation and market uncertainty. This asset class is best for investors looking for safe havens during times of volatility. Gold has historically offered moderate returns and has proven to be a stable store of value. Risk levels are relatively low to moderate, making it a solid addition to a diversified portfolio.

Cryptocurrencies: Digital currencies like Bitcoin, Ethereum, and others use blockchain technology. While this asset class has the potential for high returns, it is accompanied by extremely high risk due to its volatility. Cryptocurrency is best suited for investors with a high-risk tolerance and a keen interest in the future of technology and digital finance.

One of the keys to successful investing is understanding the relationship between your age and your investment strategy. The goal is to align your asset allocation with your risk tolerance, investment horizon, and financial objectives.

so lets see asset allocation based on the age,

Age 20-30: Focus on growth-oriented investments like stocks, mutual funds, and possibly cryptocurrencies. You have more time to ride out market fluctuations, so you can afford to take on more risk. The longer your investment horizon, the greater the potential for compounding growth.

Age 30-40: Start diversifying your portfolio by adding mutual funds, bonds, and real estate. Continue holding some equities for growth but balance with more conservative investments to mitigate risk. As you approach middle age, it's wise to build a more stable portfolio that can provide a balance between growth and security.

Age 40-50: Shift focus towards more conservative investments such as bonds, mutual funds, and real estate. Reduce exposure to high-risk equities and focus on stable, income-generating assets. This stage is about preparing for retirement by gradually moving towards more stable and lower-risk investments.

Age 50-60: At this stage, your primary goal should be to preserve your wealth. Focus on conservative investments like bonds, real estate, and low-risk mutual funds. Gold and other safe-haven assets can help protect your investments from potential market downturns. Preserve your capital while still keeping some avenues open for moderate returns.

The key to successful investing lies in aligning your asset allocation with your age, risk tolerance, and investment horizon. Starting early is essential because it allows the power of compounding to work its magic. As time goes on, your strategy should become more conservative to protect your investments. Remember, the right approach will depend on your individual circumstances, but having a well-rounded, diversified portfolio will help you navigate the ups and downs of the investment landscape with greater confidence.Now lets learn how you can build your own portfolio with the help of all the asset classes available.

The Art of building your portfolio:

Building an investment portfolio is like creating a recipe for your financial future. You mix different ingredients (or investments) in the right amounts to achieve the best outcome. While there's a bit of strategy and planning involved, the main goal is to make sure your money grows over time and stays safe. In this chapter, we'll walk through how to build your portfolio in a simple, straightforward way.

Now you will be having a question in your mind whats is a portfolio?

Think of a portfolio as a collection of all the investments you own. This can include stocks, bonds, real estate, and other assets. Your portfolio is there to help you achieve your financial goals—whether that's saving for retirement, buying a home, or funding your children's education.

The Basics of Asset allocation is all about deciding how to divide your money between different types of investments. The goal is to find the right balance between risk and reward. For example:

Risky assets like stocks offer the chance for big growth but can also go up and down a lot.
Safer assets like bonds provide more stable, predictable returns.

The mix you choose depends on how much risk you're comfortable with and how long you plan to invest.

we need to diversify our portfolio Don't Put All Your Eggs in One Basket Diversification means spreading your investments across different areas so that if one part doesn't perform well, others might do better. This can include:

Different types of investments (stocks, bonds, real estate, etc.)
Different industries (like technology, healthcare, or energy)
Different regions (domestic vs. international markets)
Diversification helps reduce the risk of losing money and can give your portfolio a better chance to grow steadily over time.

Keeping Things on Track Over time, some investments in your portfolio will do better than others. Rebalancing means adjusting your portfolio back to your original plan, ensuring that no one type of investment becomes too large or too small. This helps you stay aligned with your goals and risk tolerance.

Here is a simple approach to build your portfolio

Evaluate Your Situation: Take a look at your current finances—your income, expenses, debt, and savings. Know what your goals are.

Choose Your Investments: Based on your goals and risk tolerance, pick a mix of investments that suit you. This might include stocks, bonds, and real estate.

Diversify: Don't put all your money into one type of investment. Spread it out to manage risk.

Set Regular Contributions: Try to invest consistently, even in small amounts. Over time, these regular contributions can make a big difference.

Review and Adjust: Keep an eye on your portfolio and make changes as needed. Life changes and market fluctuations may require you to rebalance your investments.

> *Building your portfolio is about finding a mix of investments that align with your goals and risk tolerance. The key is to start early, stay consistent, and adjust over time. With a little patience and regular attention, your portfolio can grow into a powerful tool to help you achieve*

your financial dreams. Remember, investing is a long-term game, and by following these simple steps, you'll be well on your way to building a strong and diversified portfolio.

INSURANCE

" Protecting Your Future "

Having insurance is essential for securing your financial well-being. In previous discussions, we've emphasized the importance of building an emergency fund, saving, and investing. Another critical aspect of financial planning is insurance, as it provides peace of mind and protection. Once these components are in place, we can confidently say we are on the path to true financial freedom.

Insurance plays a crucial role in safeguarding your financial goals, even in your absence. If something unfortunate happens to you before your investments have matured, insurance ensures that your goals are still met, and your dependents continue to receive the necessary financial support. This is the primary purpose of having insurance.

Now, let's explore the types of insurance you should consider to protect yourself and your dependents.

Life Insurance

Life insurance is a must-have for anyone with dependents. In the event of your untimely passing, it ensures that your loved ones are financially protected. From covering daily household expenses to funding your children's education or paying off debts, life insurance provides the financial stability your family will need.
Why Is Life Insurance Important?

Life insurance is not about planning for death; it's about safeguarding life. It provides your family with the financial stability to:

Maintain their lifestyle:
Covers daily living expenses like rent, groceries, and utilities.

Secure your children's future:
Funds education and other long-term goals.
Pay off liabilities:
Ensures debts like home loans or personal loans don't burden your family.
Handle unforeseen expenses:
Covers immediate needs such as medical bills or funeral costs.

Common Misconceptions About Life Insurance

"I'm too young to need life insurance."

Many believe life insurance is only necessary later in life. However, buying it early can lock in lower premiums and ensure you are covered when you need it most.

"I can't afford life insurance."

In reality, there are a variety of plans to suit every budget. Term life insurance, for instance, offers high coverage at affordable rates.

"I don't need it because I'm healthy."

Good health today doesn't guarantee immunity from life's uncertainties. Life insurance is about preparing for the unexpected.

lets see some types of Life Insurance availabel

Term Life Insurance:

Pure protection plan that provides coverage for a specific term.
Affordable premiums and high sum assured.
Ideal for covering critical financial milestones like mortgage repayment or children's education.

Whole Life Insurance:

Offers lifelong coverage and builds cash value over time.
Can serve as a long-term savings instrument alongside protection.

Unit-Linked Insurance Plans (ULIPs):

Combines life coverage with investment options.
Allows you to grow wealth while staying insured.

Endowment Plans:

Provides life coverage and a lump sum payout at maturity.
Suitable for those looking for a disciplined savings plan.

◆ ◆ ◆

DEBT FREE

"The Path to a Debt-Free Life"

The Road to Financial Freedom: Becoming Debt-Free

Living a debt-free life is not just about numbers—it's about reclaiming your peace of mind and the freedom to pursue your dreams without financial burdens. While the journey may seem challenging, with discipline and a clear strategy, anyone can achieve a debt-free lifestyle. Let's explore the steps to break free from the shackles of debt.

"Acknowledge Your Debt"

The first step to becoming debt-free is understanding the full scope of your financial obligations. Create a comprehensive list of all your debts—credit cards, personal loans, student loans, or outstanding bills. For each, note the balance, interest rate, and minimum payment. This clarity is crucial for forming an effective repayment strategy.

A realistic budget is your most powerful tool in eliminating debt. Analyze your income and expenses to identify areas where you can cut back. Allocate a specific portion of your budget exclusively for debt repayment, and ensure you're spending less than you earn each month.

Two popular methods can guide your repayment journey:

The Snowball Method: Pay off the smallest debt first while making minimum payments on others. This builds momentum and motivation as you see progress quickly.

The Avalanche Method: Focus on debts with the highest interest rates first to save more money in the long run.

Breaking the cycle of debt requires discipline. Put your credit cards on hold, and avoid taking out new loans unless absolutely necessary. Shift to using cash or debit for purchases to maintain control over your spending.

Paying off debt faster often requires an increase in income. Consider taking up a side hustle, freelancing, or selling unused items to generate extra funds. Direct any bonuses, tax refunds, or unexpected windfalls toward your debt repayment plan.

One of the main reasons people fall into debt is the lack of an emergency fund. Start by setting aside a small amount—such as $1,000—for unexpected expenses. Once you're debt-free, expand this fund to cover three to six months of living expenses to safeguard your financial stability.

Reflect on what led to your debt in the first place. Was it impulsive spending? Lack of financial literacy? Understanding these patterns will help you avoid repeating them and maintain a debt-free lifestyle.
Debt freedom isn't just about paying off balances—it's about what lies beyond. Visualize your goals: owning a home, starting a business, traveling the world, or saving for retirement. Let these dreams inspire you to stay the course.

Becoming debt-free is a transformative journey that goes beyond money. It's about regaining control, reducing stress, and unlocking opportunities for growth and happiness. With a clear plan and unwavering commitment, you can break free from debt and write the next chapter of your life with confidence and purpose.

MOHAMMED RAHISH

CONCLUSION

As you reach the end of this book, you stand at the threshold of a new chapter in your financial journey. The knowledge you've gained—about budgeting, saving, investing, managing debt, and protecting your future—has the power to transform the way you approach money. But knowledge alone is not enough. To truly take control of your finances and achieve financial freedom, action is required.

The principles outlined here are not one-time solutions but lifelong habits that, when practiced consistently, will set you on a course for long-term success. Financial freedom isn't just about accumulating wealth; it's about creating a sense of security, having the freedom to pursue your passions, and living a life free from financial stress. It's about building a future where you can thrive, not just survive.

Remember, the journey to financial independence is not a sprint but a marathon. It will require patience, discipline, and perseverance. But by taking small, deliberate steps every day, you'll make significant progress over time. Start by applying what you've learned, stay focused on your goals, and adjust as needed along the way.

Along this journey, you may encounter challenges—unexpected expenses, market fluctuations, or personal setbacks. But each of these is an opportunity to learn, grow, and adapt. Keep your eyes on the bigger picture and stay committed to your vision of financial freedom.

Above all, trust in your ability to create the financial future you deserve. The tools are in your hands, and now it's up to you to use them. Financial independence is within reach, and with determination, you can build the life of your dreams.

Thank you for joining me on this journey. May your path to financial freedom be prosperous, fulfilling, and full of possibilities.

Your financial future starts today. Take the first step.

www.ingramcontent.com/pod-product-compliance
Lightning Source LLC
Chambersburg PA
CBHW030103230526
45471CB00003B/1227